GREAT MINDS® WIT & WISDOM

Grade 3 Module 3
A New Home

Student Edition

GREAT MINDS™

Great Minds® is the creator of *Eureka Math*®,
Wit & Wisdom®, *Alexandria Plan*™, and *PhD Science*®.

Published by Great Minds PBC
greatminds.org

Printed in the USA

A-Print

2 3 4 5 6 7 8 9 10 CCR 27 26 25 24

979-8-88588-742-7

Student Edition

Name

Handout 1A:
Model Introductory Paragraph

Directions:

1. Circle the part of the introduction that catches the reader's attention.

2. In the blank column, explain how that part of the introduction catches the reader's attention.

3. Underline the topic of the essay.

4. In the blank column, explain how we know the topic of the essay.

5. In the blank column, write a "1" next to the first important point, a "2" next to the second important point, and a "3" next to the third important point.

Why would a person leave his home, friends, and family to make a long, dangerous trip across the ocean and begin a new life in a strange country? For some, coming to America was a great adventure; for others, it was scary. There were many reasons that people made the decision to leave home. Many people left for America because they needed jobs. Some immigrants left for the United States because there was a famine in Europe. For others, there was little land to farm or live on, so people ended up in overcrowded conditions.

Name

Handout 1B:
A Postcard to Grandfather

Directions: Review the passage you read with your group. Then write a postcard to Grandfather telling him one thing you noticed and asking him one question you wondered about while reading *Grandfather's Journey*. Use the sentence frames that follow to help you. When you have finished, illustrate your postcard to show a place described in the passage you read.

Dear Grandfather,

_____

_____

_____

_____

_____

_____

Love,

_____

Sentence frames that might help you:

- **One thing I noticed was _____. This makes me think**

  _____.

- **One thing I wondered was _____. I wish I knew**

  _____.

Name

Handout 1C: Reading Log

Directions: Track your daily reading by recording the date, genre, title and author, and how many pages you read.

Date	Literature (L) or Informational (I) Text	Title and Author	Pages Read

Name

Handout 1D: Fluency Homework

Directions:

1. Day 1: Read the text carefully, and annotate to help you read fluently.

2. Each day:

   a. Practice reading the text aloud three to five times.

   b. Evaluate your progress by placing a √+, √, or √- in the appropriate, unshaded box.

   c. Ask someone (adult or peer) to listen and evaluate you as well.

3. Last day: Answer the self-reflection questions at the end.

Grandfather's Journey

by Allen Say

As his daughter grew, my grandfather began to think about his own childhood. He thought about his old friends. He remembered the mountains and rivers of his home. He surrounded himself with songbirds, but he could not forget. Finally, when his daughter was nearly grown, he could wait no more. He took his family and returned to his homeland. Once again he saw the mountains and rivers of his childhood. They were just as he had remembered them. Once again he exchanged stories and laughed with his old friends. ... He raised warblers and silvereyes, but he could not forget the mountains and rivers of California.

Say, Allen. *Grandfather's Journey.* Houghton Mifflin Company, 1993, pp. 17–25.

Student Performance Checklist	Day 1		Day 2		Day 3		Day 4	
	You	Listener*	You	Listener*	You	Listener*	You	Listener*
Accurately read the passage three to five times.								
Read with appropriate phrasing and pausing.								
Read with appropriate expression.								
Read articulately at a good pace and an audible volume.								

*Adult or peer

Self-reflection: What choices did you make when deciding how to read this passage, and why? What would you like to improve on or try differently next time? (Thoughtfully answer these questions below.)

Name

Handout 3A:
Speaking and Listening Checklist

Directions: Evaluate your speaking and listening skills by marking + for "yes" and Δ for "not yet" in the appropriate boxes. Then ask a classmate to evaluate how well you used the skills. Your teacher will complete the third column, based on what they observe.

	Self +/ Δ	Peer +/ Δ	Teacher +/ Δ
• I prepared for my discussion.			
• I read the material before discussing it.			
• I selected details from the text to include in the discussion.			
• I identified points of interest and/or confusion.			
• I listened actively.			
• I listened for key words.			
• I linked my comments to other people's comments.			
• My comments showed that I am curious about what we are learning.			
• My comments showed that I can recount what others say.			

• I followed all the rules for working in a small group.			
• I took turns speaking and listening.			
• I asked thoughtful questions.			
• I asked and answered questions to check understanding.			
• I asked and answered questions to stay on topic.			
• I asked and answered questions to elaborate on a topic.			
• I agreed and disagreed respectfully.			
• I used a polite tone of voice throughout the discussion.			
• I used a sentence stem to help me agree or disagree respectfully.			
• I used a nonverbal cue to show that I agreed or disagreed with a speaker.			
• I explained my thinking in light of our discussion.			
• I used appropriate facts and details to report on a topic or text.			
• I spoke clearly at an understandable pace.			
Total number of +'s:			

Name
_____

Handout 3B: Writing Planner

Directions: Use this graphic organizer to plan a response to the following prompt:

Consider everything that you have learned about Grandfather from reading _Grandfather's Journey._ Does Grandfather change during the story? Write an essay explaining your answer.

H	Hook the Reader	
I	Introduce your reader to the topic.	
T	Topic—What is the important idea, and what are the supporting points?	

Body Paragraph 1

T	Topic Statement	
	Linking Word	
E	Evidence (Fact, Definition, or Detail)	
E	Elaboration	
C	Concluding Statement	

Body Paragraph 2		
	Linking Word	
T	Topic Statement	
E	Evidence (Fact, Definition, or Detail)	
E	Elaboration	
	Linking Word	
C	Concluding Statement	

Conclusion

Name

Handout 5A:
Comparison and Contrast Essay

Directions: Read the comparison and contrast essay below. Use yellow to highlight sentences that show similarities between Japan and the United States. Use blue to highlight differences between the two countries.

The narrator's grandfather in *Grandfather's Journey* by Allen Say is a man who wanted to see the world. He went to live in the United States. Grandfather loved it there, but one day he decided to go back to Japan. There were many things that were similar between the United States and Japan. There were also many things that were different.

One thing that was similar is that Japan and the United States both have mountains and rivers. When Grandfather was in California, he missed the mountains and rivers in Japan. Similarly, when Grandfather was in Japan, he missed the mountains and rivers in California. Grandfather loved both places.

Even though there were many things that were alike, there were also many things that were different. When Grandfather lived in California he lived in a big city and wore European clothes. However, in Japan he lived in a small village and wore a kimono. When Grandfather was in California, he met many people. On the other hand, when he was in Japan, he saw the old friends that he missed.

Grandfather loved both the United States and Japan. He wanted to return to the United States one day, but he never did.

Name

Handout 5B: Using Singular and Plural Possessive Nouns

Directions: Read the narrative below. Then form the singular or plural possessive of the nouns in the Word Bank to complete the story.

My grandfather was a young man when he left his home in Japan and went to see the world. _____ journey began on a steamship. The _____ size astonished him. The _____ huge curves made him think of a woodcut he had once seen. He explored North America by train and riverboat. He visited many cities. The _____ shining towers always surprised him. He shook many _____ hands and visited many _____ homes. The more he traveled, the more he longed to see new places. He never thought of returning home. Of all the places he visited, he liked California best. He loved the lonely _____ strong sunlight. He made his home by the San Francisco Bay.

Word Bank
Grandfather
ocean
wave
city
man
person
seacoast

Name

Handout 6A: Comparison and Contrast Sentence Frames

Directions: Reread pages 29–31 of *Grandfather's Journey*. How are Grandfather and the narrator similar and how are they different?

In *Grandfather's Journey*, by Allen Say, Grandfather and the

narrator are alike. For example, they both _____

_____.

They are also similar because they both _____

_____.

On the other hand, the two characters are different because

Grandfather _____,

but the narrator _____.

Another difference is that Grandfather _____,

while the narrator _____.

Name

Handout 7A:
Comparison and Contrast Essay

Directions: Read the comparison and contrast essay below. Use yellow to highlight sentences that show similarities between Japan and the United States. Use blue to highlight differences between the two countries.

In *Tea with Milk*, by Allen Say, Masako was a young woman who moved from San Francisco to Japan. At first she was unhappy in Japan, but Masako made a life for herself there. She found some things that were similar to her old life, but there were also many differences.

One thing that was similar was that Osaka and San Francisco were both big cities. Osaka had many cars, just like San Francisco. Similarly, the city noises in Osaka reminded Masako of the sounds of San Francisco. Masako was happy to be in a big city again.

Even though Masako was happy to be in the big city of Osaka, she noticed many differences between life in Japan and life in the US. In Japan, people were surprised that Masako could drive a car. However, in the US, many women drove cars. Another difference Masako discovered was that in Japan, it was shameful for women to work. On the other hand, in the US, Masako had planned on going to college and getting a job.

Masako found a way to be happy in her new home. It was not easy at first, but in the end, Masako decided not to return to the US.

Name

Handout 7B: Postcard to Masako

Directions: Think about what you noticed and wondered as you read and listened to *Tea with Milk*. Then write a postcard to Masako telling her one detail you noticed that helped you understand the story better. Then ask her one question you wondered about. Use the sentence frames below to help you. When you have finished, illustrate your postcard.

Dear Masako,

_____

_____

_____

_____

_____

      Sincerely, _____

Sentence frames that might help you:

- **One thing I noticed was** _____. **This makes me think** _____.

- **One thing I wondered was** _____. **I wish I knew** _____.

Name

Handout 7C: Fluency Homework

Directions:

1. Day 1: Read the text carefully, and annotate to help you read fluently.

2. Each day:

   a. Practice reading the text aloud three to five times.

   b. Evaluate your progress by placing a √+, √, or √- in the appropriate, unshaded box.

   c. Ask someone (adult or peer) to listen and evaluate you as well.

3. Last day: Answer the self-reflection questions at the end.

Tea with Milk
by Allen Say

Once they arrived in Japan, she felt even worse. Her new home was drafty, with windows made of paper. She had to wear kimonos and sit on floors until her legs went numb. No one called her May, and Masako sounded like someone else's name. There were no more pancakes or omelets, fried chicken or spaghetti. I'll never get used to this place, she thought with a heavy heart.

Worst of all, Masako had to attend high school all over again. To learn her own language, her mother said. She could not make friends with any of the other students; they called her *gaijin* and laughed at her. *Gaijin* means "foreigner."

Say, Allen. *Tea with Milk.* Houghton Mifflin Company, 1999, pp. 6–7.

Student Performance Checklist	Day 1		Day 2		Day 3		Day 4	
	You	Listener*	You	Listener*	You	Listener*	You	Listener*
Accurately read the passage three to five times.								
Read with appropriate phrasing and pausing.								
Read with appropriate expression.								
Read articulately at a good pace and an audible volume.								

*Adult or peer

Self-reflection: What choices did you make when deciding how to read this passage, and why? What would you like to improve on or try differently next time? (Thoughtfully answer these questions below.)

Name

Handout 8B: Speaking and Listening Process Checklist

Directions: Use the checklist below to monitor how well you used your speaking and listening skills. Then ask a classmate to evaluate how well you used the skills. Your teacher will complete the third column, based on what they observe.

	Self +/ Δ	Peer +/ Δ	Teacher +/ Δ
• I prepared for my discussion.			
• I read the material before discussing it.			
• I selected details from the text to include during the discussion.			
• I identified points of interest and/or confusion.			
• I listened actively.			
• I listened for key words.			
• I linked my comments to comments from other people.			
• My comments showed that I am curious about what we are learning.			
• My comments showed that I can recount what others say.			

• I followed all the rules for working in a small group.			
• I took turns speaking and listening.			
• I asked thoughtful questions.			
• I asked and answered questions to check understanding.			
• I asked and answered questions to stay on topic.			
• I asked and answered questions to elaborate on a topic.			
• I agreed and disagreed respectfully.			
• I used a polite tone of voice throughout the discussion.			
• I used a sentence stem to help me agree or disagree respectfully.			
• I used a nonverbal cue to show that I agreed or disagreed with a speaker.			
• I explained my thinking in light of our discussion.			
• I used appropriate facts and details to report on a topic or text.			
• I spoke clearly at an understandable pace.			

Name

Handout 8C: Subject-Verb Agreement

Directions:

1. Read the following passage adapted from *Tea with Milk*.

2. Find the subject in each sentence or phrase. Highlight all of the <u>singular subjects</u> in one color and all of the <u>plural subjects</u> in another color.

3. Find the verb in each sentence or phrase. Highlight all of the <u>singular verbs</u> in one color. Highlight all of the <u>plural verbs</u> in another color.

So they were married in Yokohama. I was their first child.

My father called my mother May. Everyone else called her Masako. At home they spoke English to each other. They spoke Japanese to me. Sometimes my mother wore a kimono, but she never got used to sitting on the floor for very long.

All this happened a long time ago, but even today I always drink my tea with milk and sugar.

Say, Allen. *Tea with Milk.* Houghton Mifflin Company, 1999, p. 32.

Name

Handout 9A:
Speaking and Listening Checklist

Directions: Evaluate your speaking and listening skills by marking + for "yes" and Δ for "not yet" in the appropriate boxes. Then ask a classmate to evaluate how well you used the skills. Your teacher will complete the third column, based on what they observe.

	Self +/ Δ	Peer +/ Δ	Teacher +/ Δ
• I prepared for my discussion.			
• I read the material before discussing it.			
• I selected details from the text to include during the discussion.			
• I identified points of interest and/or confusion.			
• I listened actively.			
• I listened for key words.			
• I linked my comments to comments from other people.			
• My comments showed that I am curious about what we are learning.			
• My comments showed that I can recount what others say.			

• I followed all the rules for working in a small group.			
• I took turns speaking and listening.			
• I asked thoughtful questions.			
• I asked and answered questions to check understanding.			
• I asked and answered questions to stay on topic.			
• I asked and answered questions to elaborate on a topic.			
• I agreed and disagreed respectfully.			
• I used a polite tone of voice throughout the discussion.			
• I used a sentence stem to help me agree or disagree respectfully.			
• I used a nonverbal cue to show that I agreed or disagreed with a speaker.			
• I explained my thinking in light of our discussion.			
• I used appropriate facts and details to report on a topic or text.			
• I spoke clearly at an understandable pace.			
• **Total number of +'s:**			

Name

Handout 10A: Masako's Point of View

Directions: Review *Tea with Milk* in your group to find evidence that Masako does or does <u>not</u> like living in Japan. Record the evidence and the page number where you found the evidence.

Page Number	Evidence That Masako Does <u>Not</u> Want to Live in Japan	Evidence That Masako Does Want to Live in Japan

Name

Handout 10B: Speaking and Listening Process Checklist

Directions: Evaluate your speaking and listening skills by marking + for "yes" and Δ for "not yet" in the appropriate boxes. Then ask a classmate to evaluate how well you used the skills. Your teacher will complete the third column, based on what they observe.

	Self +/ Δ	Peer +/ Δ	Teacher +/ Δ
• I prepared for my discussion.			
• I read the material before discussing it.			
• I selected details from the text to include during the discussion.			
• I identified points of interest and/or confusion.			
• I listened actively.			
• I listened for key words.			
• I linked my comments to comments from other people.			
• My comments showed that I am curious about what we are learning.			
• My comments showed that I can recount what others say.			

• I followed all the rules for working in a small group.			
• I took turns speaking and listening.			
• I asked thoughtful questions.			
• I asked and answered questions to check understanding.			
• I asked and answered questions to stay on topic.			
• I asked and answered questions to elaborate on a topic.			
• I agreed and disagreed respectfully.			
• I used a polite tone of voice throughout the discussion.			
• I used a sentence stem to help me agree or disagree respectfully.			
• I used a nonverbal cue to show that I agreed or disagreed with a speaker.			
• I explained my thinking in light of our discussion.			
• I used appropriate facts and details to report on a topic or text.			
• I spoke clearly at an understandable pace.			
• **Total number of +'s:**			

Name

Handout 10C: Socratic Seminar Participation Guidelines

Directions: Follow the directions below as you participate in the Socratic Seminar.

- Prepare for the seminar by reviewing the texts, your notes, and charts or resources that will help you discuss the prompt.

- Take turns speaking.

- Listen carefully to others by tracking the speaker.

- Speak at least once.

- Speak to each other, not to the teacher, by turning your eyes and bodies toward one another.

- Ask questions.

- Stay on topic.

Ways to Participate in Socratic Seminar

- Take a risk.

- Ask a question.

- Ask a follow-up question.

- Practice active listening.

- Provide evidence.

- Smile and have fun.

- Stay focused.

Name

Handout 10D:
Socratic Seminar 1 Self-Assessment

Directions: Complete this chart by using one of the letters from the key to describe how often you performed the action described. In the last column, explain why you selected the letter you did.

A = I always did that.　　**S** = I sometimes did that.　　**N** = I'll do that next time.

Expectation	Evaluation (A, S, N)	Evidence: Why did you choose that rating?
I came to the seminar prepared and used my work as I participated in the seminar.		
I followed our class rules for the seminar.		
I referred to evidence in the text when asking and answering questions.		
I used evidence from the text to elaborate on my ideas.		
I spoke in complete sentences.		
I asked questions to stay on topic.		
I asked and answered questions to provide more details.		

Name

Handout 11A: Repetition Analysis

Directions: Reread the pages below. Then reread the sentences below. In your group, explain why each sentence is important. Then use your analysis to answer the question at the bottom of the page.

Page Number	Sentence	Why the Sentence Is Important
4	At her friends' houses she ate pancakes and muffins and drank tea with milk and sugar.	
10	And I like my tea with milk and sugar!	
26	"Did you always drink tea with milk and sugar?"	
32	All of this happened a long time ago, but even today I always drink my tea with milk and sugar.	

Why is "tea with milk and sugar" important to Masako?

"Tea with milk and sugar" is important to Masako because _____

_____.

Name

Handout 11B:
Dialogue from *Tea with Milk*

Directions: Follow along as the group reads Passage 1 for the class.

If you are reading for the class, highlight the name of the character you will be in the performance. Then highlight the words you will speak. Read aloud your dialogue when it is your turn.

After the class reads Passage 1 together, independently read Passage 2 and follow these steps:

1. Highlight the exact words that a character speaks.

2. Circle and label speaker tags you notice.

3. Circle and label quotation marks.

4. Circle and label punctuation that helps you read the dialogue.

Passage 1:

| Masako | Little boy | Englishwoman | Narrator |

In the afternoon, as she brought down the elevator, she noticed that a small crowd had gathered in the lobby. In the middle stood the supervisor, bowing and waving his arms at the family. Suddenly Masako flushed with excitement. The family was speaking English!

"Can I be of any help?" Masako asked from behind the crowd.

"You sound like an American," a little boy said.

Say, Allen. *Tea with Milk.* Houghton Mifflin Company, 1999, p. 22.

Passage 2:

One night in the late fall they had dinner at a restaurant they liked. After a while May noticed that she was doing all the talking and Joseph was not eating his food.

"Are you all right?" she asked. Joseph nodded but said nothing.

As they left the restaurant, May said, "Tell me what's wrong."

"They are transferring me," Joseph said.

"What?"

"They are sending me to another office."

"Where?"

"Yokohama."

"No!"

Say, Allen. *Tea with Milk*. Houghton Mifflin Company, 1999, p. 28.

Name

Handout 12A: Writing Planner

Directions: Use this graphic organizer to plan a response to Focusing Question Task 1.

Hook:

Introduction (Text and Author):

Background:

Topic Sentence:

One important similarity between Grandfather and

Masako's experiences as immigrants:

Example from *Grandfather's Journey*:

Example from *Tea with Milk*:

Topic Sentence:

One important difference between Grandfather and Masako's experiences as immigrants:

Example from *Grandfather's Journey*:

Example from *Tea with Milk*:

Conclusion (What do the two stories help readers understand about the experiences of immigration?):

Name

Handout 12B: Punctuating Dialogue

Directions: Work with a partner to read the following conversation between Joseph and Masako aloud. Alternate readers each time the speaker changes.

They met later and had tea in a nearby café. Well, Miss Moriwaki, Joseph said, looking at Masako's business card. I'd like if you'd call me May, she said. Did you always drink tea with milk and sugar? It's how we used to have it at school, with crumpets, he said. So what brings you to the store three mornings running? Joseph laughed. I work for Hong Kong and Shanghai Bank. I was transferred here six months ago and I haven't had a real conversation since. Then I heard you speaking English at the store the other day. What a patient man you are, she said laughing. And I'm glad you came back. This is the first real conversation I've had in a whole year.

Say, Allen. *Tea with Milk*. Houghton Mifflin Company, 1999, p. 26.

Name

Handout 13A:
Focusing Question Task 1 Checklist

Directions: Use this checklist to revise your writing. Mark + for "yes" and Δ for "not yet." Ask someone (adult or peer) to evaluate your writing as well.

Reading Comprehension	Self +/ Δ	Peer +/ Δ	Teacher +/ Δ
• My writing shows I understand the main idea in a text.			
• I completed a graphic organizer comparing and contrasting two stories by Allen Say.			
• I describe the challenges related to immigration that characters face in Allen Say's stories.			
• I compared and contrasted the characters from two stories by Allen Say.			
Structure			
• I respond to all parts of the prompt.			
• I focus on my topic.			
• I introduce the topic in my introductory paragraph.			
• I organize information about my topic into groups.			

• My concluding section refers to my topic.			
• I use at least three linking words and phrases to connect ideas.			
Development			
• I develop my topic with evidence from the text.			
• My evidence is related to the topic.			
• I elaborate upon evidence by explaining it.			
Style			
• I use vocabulary words that are appropriate to the topic.			
• I use and circle at least three new vocabulary words.			
• My writing is appropriate for the purpose and audience of the task.			
Conventions			
• I ensure subject-verb agreement.			
Writing Process			
• I use a Writing Planner to organize my ideas.			
• I provide thoughtful feedback in peer revision.			
• I use feedback in peer revision.			
Total number of +'s:			

Name

Handout 14A: Focusing Question Task 1 Revision Checklist

Directions:

1. Exchange Focusing Question Task 1 essays with a partner.

2. Read the essay in its entirety once before making comments or suggestions.

3. For each sentence, put one finger on the subject and another finger on the verb.

4. Write <u>s/v</u> in the margin next to a sentence that does <u>not</u> use subject-verb agreement.

5. Complete the checklist on the back of this handout.

6. Return the essay and checklist to your partner.

7. Review and revise your own essay, using your partner's feedback.

Writer:_____   Editor:_____

In the essay, the writer ...	Yes	Sometimes	Rarely	Not Present
Ensures subject-verb agreement.				
The best part of the essay is ...				
A suggestion to make the essay even better is ...				

Name

Handout 16A: Fluency Homework

Directions:

1. Day 1: Read the text carefully, and annotate to help you read fluently.

2. Each day:

   a. Practice reading the text aloud three to five times.

   b. Evaluate your progress by placing a √+, √, or √- in the appropriate, unshaded box.

   c. Ask someone (adult or peer) to listen and evaluate you as well.

3. Last day: Answer the self-reflection questions at the end.

Coming to America: The Story of Immigration by Betsy Maestro

Immigrants settled and farmed this land before it was a country. Others created a new nation and founded its government. Immigrants built the cities, roads and railways of America. They have toiled in its fields, its factories, and its mills. Immigrants, too, have made the music of this land, written its books, and recorded its beauty in paintings. The spirit of American strength and independence is the spirit of its people—the spirit of its immigrants and their children.

Maestro, Betsy. *Coming to America: The Story of Immigration.* Illustrated by Susannah Ryan.

Scholastic, 1996, p. 37.

Student Performance Checklist	Day 1		Day 2		Day 3		Day 4	
	You	Listener*	You	Listener*	You	Listener*	You	Listener*
Accurately read the passage three to five times.								
Read with appropriate phrasing and pausing.								
Read with appropriate expression.								
Read articulately at a good pace and an audible volume.								

*Adult or peer

Self-reflection: What choices did you make when deciding how to read this passage, and why? What would you like to improve on or try differently next time? (Thoughtfully answer these questions below.)

Name

Handout 16B:
Using Commas in Addresses

Directions: Read each address below. Circle the commas you notice. Below each address, write the name of the city and the name of the state.

Houghton Mifflin Company

215 Park Avenue South

New York, New York 10003

City: _____

State: _____

Children's Press

95 Madison Avenue

New York, New York 10016

City: _____

State: _____

Allen Say

222 Berkeley St.

Boston, Massachusetts 02116

City: _____

State: _____

National Japanese American Historical Society

1684 Post Street

San Francisco, California 94115

City: _____

State: _____

King Ranch

Three Riverway Street

Houston, Texas 77056

City: _____

State: _____

Name

Handout 18A: ESCAPE into the Story Graphic Organizer

Directions: Use this graphic organizer to plan a story about an illustration in *Coming to America: The Story of Immigration.*

	E	Establish	How will you orient your reader to the situation? (Explain what happens.)
	S	Setting	When and where does the story take place?
	C	Characters	Who is the story about, and what do they want?
	A	Action	What events happen, and how do the characters respond?
	P	Problem	What prevents the main character from getting what they want?
	E	Ending	What is the resolution to the problem?

Name

Handout 19A: Frayer Model

Directions: With a partner, create a Frayer Model for the word <u>native</u> using the graphic organizer below.

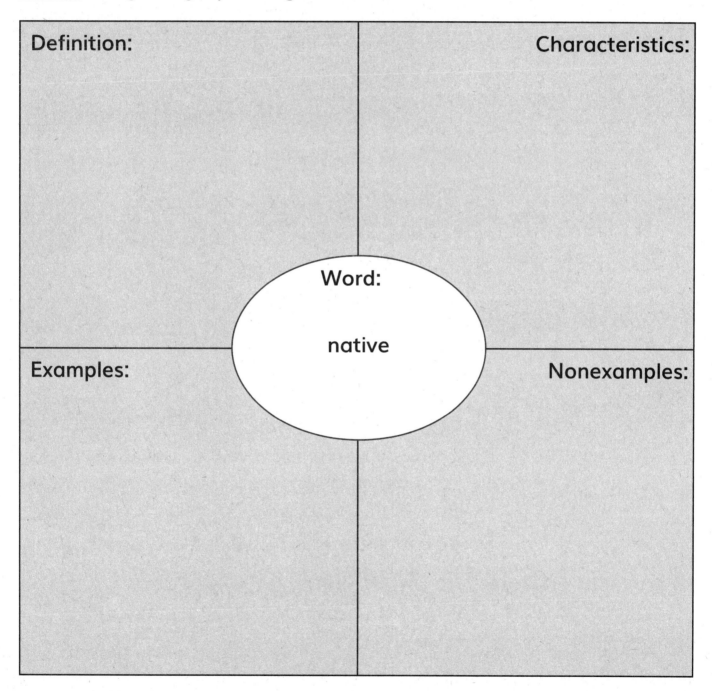

Name

Handout 22A: "The New Colossus"

Directions: "The New Colossus," by Emma Lazarus, describes the Statue of Liberty. A copy of the poem was added to the Statue of Liberty in 1903. Circle words or phrases that describe the Statue of Liberty as you listen to the poem read aloud.

The New Colossus
by Emma Lazarus

Not like the brazen giant of Greek fame,

With conquering limbs astride from land to land;

Here at our sea-washed, sunset gates shall stand

A mighty woman with a torch, whose flame

Is the imprisoned lightning, and her name

Mother of Exiles. From her beacon-hand

Glows world-wide welcome; her mild eyes command

The air-bridged harbor that twin cities frame.

"Keep, ancient lands, your storied pomp!" cries she

With silent lips. "Give me your tired, your poor,

Your huddled masses yearning to breathe free,

The wretched refuse of your teeming shore.

Send these, the homeless, tempest-tost to me,

I lift my lamp beside the golden door!"

Name

Handout 22B:
Speaking and Listening Checklist

Directions: Evaluate your speaking and listening skills by marking +
for "yes" and Δ for "not yet" in the appropriate boxes. Then ask a
classmate to evaluate how well you used the skills. Your teacher will
complete the third column, based on what they observe.

	Self +/ Δ	Peer +/ Δ	Teacher +/ Δ
• I prepared for my discussion.			
• I read the material before discussing it.			
• I selected details from the text to include during the discussion.			
• I identified points of interest and/or confusion.			
• I listened actively.			
• I listened for key words.			
• I linked my comments to comments from other people.			
• My comments showed that I am curious about what we are learning.			
• My comments showed that I can recount what others say.			

• I followed all the rules for working in a small group.			
• I took turns speaking and listening.			
• I asked thoughtful questions.			
• I asked and answered questions to check understanding.			
• I asked and answered questions to stay on topic.			
• I asked and answered questions to elaborate on a topic.			
• I agreed and disagreed respectfully.			
• I used a polite tone of voice throughout the discussion.			
• I used a sentence stem to help me agree or disagree respectfully.			
• I used a nonverbal cue to show that I agreed or disagreed with a speaker.			
• I explained my thinking in light of our discussion.			
• I used appropriate facts and details to report on a topic or text.			
• I spoke clearly at an understandable pace.			
Total number of +'s:			

Name

Handout 22C:
Socratic Seminar 2 Self-Assessment

Directions: Complete this chart by using one of the letters from the key to describe how often you performed the described action. In the last column, explain why you selected the letter you did.

A = I always did that.   **S** = I sometimes did that.   **N** = I'll do that next time.

Expectation	Evaluation (A, S, N)	Evidence: Why did you choose that rating?
I came to the seminar prepared, and used my work as I participated in the seminar.		
I followed our class rules for the seminar.		
I referred to evidence in the text when asking and answering questions.		
I used evidence from the text to elaborate on my ideas.		
I spoke in complete sentences.		
I asked questions to stay on topic.		
I asked and answered questions to provide more details.		

Name

Handout 24A: Stationery

Directions: Use this stationery to complete Assessment 23A. Be sure to write your character's address in the upper right-hand corner. Include a greeting and a closing. Use extra paper if necessary.

_____

_____

_____

_____ ,

_____

_____

_____

_____

_____

_____

_____

Name

Handout 24B:
Focusing Question Task 2 Checklist

Directions:

1. Use this checklist as you review your completed letter. Mark + for "yes" and Δ for "not yet."

2. Then give your letter and the checklist to a peer, who will also review the checklist.

3. Make necessary revisions.

4. Give the completed letter and checklist to your teacher.

ading Comprehension	Self +/ Δ	Peer +/ Δ	Teacher +/ Δ
I e details about immigration, including in rmation about why and how a person im igrated.			
Str ture			
I re ond to all parts of the prompt.			
I us letter format to tell my story.			
I incl e a salutation in the letter.			
I incl e a closing in the letter.			
I intro ce a narrator and/or character(s).			

Development			
I establish a setting and conflict for my narrative or story.			
Style			
I use vocabulary words that are appropriate to the topic.			
I use and circle at least three new vocabulary words.			
My writing is appropriate for the purpose and audience of the task.			
Conventions			
I ensure subject-verb agreement.			
I use commas in addresses correctly.			
Research			
I include at least one detail I learned from the oral histories of real immigrants.			
Writing Process			
I use a Writing Planner to organize my ideas.			
I provide thoughtful feedback in peer revision.			
I use feedback in peer revision.			
Total number of +'s:			

Name

Handout 24C: Focusing Question Task 2 Revision Checklist

Directions:

1. Exchange Focusing Question Task 2 letters with a partner.

2. Read your partner's letter all the way through before making comments or suggestions.

3. Use proofreading marks to annotate the letter, and indicate punctuation corrections.

4. Write "s/v" in the margin next to sentences that do <u>not</u> use subject-verb agreement.

5. Complete the checklist on page 2.

6. Return the letter and checklist to your partner.

7. Review and revise your own letter, using your partner's feedback.

Writer:_____   Editor:_____

In the letter, the writer ...	Yes	Sometimes	Rarely	Not Present
Ensures subject-verb agreement.				
Uses a comma between the city and state of the address (e.g., New York City, New York).				

The best part of your letter is ...

A suggestion to make your letter even better is ...

Name

Handout 25A: Fluency Homework

Directions:

1. Day 1: Read the text carefully, and annotate to help you read fluently.

2. Each day:
   a. Practice reading the text aloud three to five times.
   b. Evaluate your progress by placing a √+, √, or √- in the appropriate, unshaded box.
   c. Ask someone (adult or peer) to listen and evaluate you as well.

3. Last day: Answer the self-reflection questions at the end.

The Keeping Quilt

by Patricia Polacco

"We will make a quilt to help us always remember home," Anna's mother said. "It will be like having the family in back home Russia dance around us at night."

And so it was. Anna's mother invited all the neighborhood ladies. They cut out animals and flowers from the scraps of clothing. Anna kept the needles threaded and handed them to the ladies as they needed them. The border of the quilt was made from Anna's babushka.

On Friday nights Anna's mother would say the prayers that started the Sabbath. The family ate challah and chicken soup. The quilt was the tablecloth.

Anna grew up and fell in love with Great-Grandpa Sasha. To show he wanted to be her husband, he gave Anna a gold coin, a dried flower, and a piece of rock salt, all tied together in a linen handkerchief. The gold was for wealth, the flower for love, and the salt so their lives would have flavor.

Polacco, Patricia. *The Keeping Quilt*. 1988. Simon & Schuster Children's Publishing Division, 2013.

Student Performance Checklist	Day 1		Day 2		Day 3		Day 4	
	You	Listener*	You	Listener*	You	Listener*	You	Listener*
Accurately read the passage three to five times.								
Read with appropriate phrasing and pausing.								
Read with appropriate expression.								
Read articulately at a good pace and an audible volume.								

*Adult or peer

Self-reflection: What choices did you make when deciding how to read this passage, and why? What would you like to improve on or try differently next time? (Thoughtfully answer these questions below.)

Name

Handout 26A: Character Chart

Directions: Review *The Keeping Quilt* and explain how each character listed in the left-hand column is related to the narrator, Patricia. Then explain how each person uses the quilt, and record important details you notice.

Character Name	Relationship to Narrator (Patricia)	How the Person Uses the Keeping Quilt	Additional Details
Anna's mother			
Anna			
Sasha			
Carle			
George			
Mary Ellen			
Patricia			
Enzo Mario			
Traci Denise			

Name

Handout 30A:
Speaking and Listening Checklist

Directions: Evaluate your speaking and listening skills by marking +
for "yes" and Δ for "not yet" in the appropriate boxes. Then ask a
classmate to evaluate how well you used the skills. Your teacher will
complete the third column, based on what they observe.

	Self +/ Δ	Peer +/ Δ	Teacher +/ Δ
• I prepared for my discussion.			
• I read the material before discussing it.			
• I selected details from the text to include during the discussion.			
• I identified points of interest and/or confusion.			
• I listened actively.			
• I listened for key words.			
• I linked my comments to comments from other people.			
• My comments showed that I am curious about what we are learning.			
• My comments showed that I can recount what others say.			

• I followed all the rules for working in a small group.			
• I took turns speaking and listening.			
• I asked thoughtful questions.			
• I asked and answered questions to check understanding.			
• I asked and answered questions to stay on topic.			
• I asked and answered questions to elaborate on a topic.			
• I agreed and disagreed respectfully.			
• I used a polite tone of voice throughout the discussion.			
• I used a sentence stem to help me agree or disagree respectfully.			
• I used a nonverbal cue to show that I agreed or disagreed with a speaker.			
• I explained my thinking in light of our discussion.			
• I used appropriate facts and details to report on a topic or text.			
• I spoke clearly at an understandable pace.			
Total number of +'s:			

Name

Handout 30B:
Socratic Seminar 3 Self-Assessment

Directions: Complete this chart by using one of the letters from the key to describe how often you performed the described action. In the last column, explain why you selected the letter you did.

A = I always did that.   **S** = I sometimes did that.   **N** = I'll do that next time.

Expectation	Evaluation (A, S, N)	Evidence: Why did you choose that rating?
I came to the seminar prepared, and used my work as I participated in the seminar.		
I followed our class rules for the seminar.		
I referred to evidence in the text when asking and answering questions.		
I used evidence from the text to elaborate on my ideas.		
I spoke in complete sentences.		
I asked questions to stay on topic.		
I asked and answered questions to provide more details.		

Name

Handout 32A: Writing Planner

Directions: Use this graphic organizer to plan a response to Focusing Question Task 30.

	E	Establish	How will you orient your reader to the situation?
	S	Setting	When and where does the story take place?
	C	Characters	Who is the story about, and what do they want?
	A	Action	What events happen, and how do the characters respond?
	P	Problem	What prevents the main character from getting what they want?
	E	Ending	What is the resolution to the problem?

Name

Handout 32B: Vocabulary Study Guide

Directions: Study the definitions, and draw a picture or write a sentence using the word to help you remember what each word means. Then glue this paper into your Vocabulary Journal.

Word	Meaning	Illustration or Sentence
liberty (n.)	Freedom.	
immigrant (n.)	Person who permanently moves to a country where they were not born.	
astonished (v.)	Surprised.	
bewildered (v.)	Confused.	
homesick (adj.)	Longing for one's home.	
longing (n.)	Desire (for something).	
shackles (n.)	Metal bands used for binding the wrists or ankles of a prisoner or animal.	
torches (n.)	Fire carried on sticks or poles as portable lights.	

foreign (adj.)	In, from, or having to do with a country that is not one's own.	
generation (n.)	People, usually in a family, born at about the same time.	
journey (n.)	Very long trip.	
bilingual (adj.)	Able to use two languages equally well.	
vermin (n.)	Unpleasant insects or small animals that can sometimes cause harm.	
ethnic (adj.)	Having to do with a large group of people with a shared culture, language, or religion, race, or national heritage.	
descendants (n.)	People related to those who lived a long time ago.	
quilt (n.)	Blanket made of pieces of fabric and featuring decorative stitching.	

Name

native (adj.)	Having to do with where a person was born.	
diadem (n.)	Crown.	
voyage (n.)	Long trip, especially by sea or through outer space.	
inspiration (n.)	Cause for or source of a new idea or feeling, usually positive.	
unique (adj.)	Having to do with qualities found in only one person, group, place, thing, or idea.	
kimono (n.)	Traditional Japanese robe-like garment with wide sleeves and a broad sash.	
ancestor (n.)	Relative who lived long ago.	
unfamiliar (adj.)	New, or not known or experienced earlier.	
childhood (n.)	Period of time when one is very young.	

nationality (n.)	Condition of being a citizen of a particular nation.	
poverty (n.)	State of being poor.	
steerage (n.)	Least expensive sleeping accommodations on a passenger ship.	
enlighten (v.)	Share knowledge.	
opportunity (n.)	Chance for something better.	

Name

Handout 33A:
Focusing Question Task 3 Checklist

Directions:

1. Use this checklist as you review your completed letter. Mark + for "yes" and Δ for "not yet."
2. Then give your letter and the checklist to a peer, who will also review the checklist.
3. Make necessary revisions.
4. Give the completed letter and checklist to your teacher.

Reading Comprehension	Self +/ Δ	Peer +/ Δ	Teacher +/ Δ
• I use details about immigration, including information about why and how a person immigrated.			
Structure			
• I respond to all parts of the prompt.			
• I introduce a narrator and/or character(s).			
• I establish setting and conflict for my narrative or story.			
• I provide a sense of closure at the end.			
• I use time words and phrases to tell my reader when events happen.			

Development			
• I use dialogue and description to develop events and characters.			
Style			
• I use vocabulary words that are appropriate to the topic.			
• I use and circle at least three new vocabulary words.			
• My writing is appropriate for the purpose and audience of the task.			
Conventions			
• I ensure subject-verb agreement.			
• I use commas in addresses correctly.			
• I form and use possessives correctly.			
Writing Process			
• I use a Writing Planner to organize my ideas.			
• I provide thoughtful feedback in peer revision.			
• I use feedback in peer revision.			
Total number of +'s:			

After completing the checklist:

1. Highlight or underline one example of dialogue that uses correct punctuation.
2. Circle one example of the correct use of possessives.
3. Write the singular and plural forms of one irregular noun you used.

Singular: _____ Plural: _____

Name

Handout 33B: Focusing Question Task 3 Revision Checklist

Directions:

1. Exchange Focusing Question Task 3 narratives with a partner.

2. Read your partner's narrative all the way through before making comments or suggestions.

3. Use proofreading marks to annotate the narrative, and indicate punctuation corrections.

4. Write "s/v" in the margin next to sentences that do not use subject-verb agreement.

5. Write "poss" in the margin next to sentences that do not use possessives correctly.

6. Complete the checklist below.

7. Return the narrative and checklist to your partner.

8. Review and revise your own narrative, using your partner's feedback.

Writer:_____   Editor:_____

In the essay, the writer ...	Yes	Sometimes	Rarely	Not Present
Uses possessives correctly.				
Ensures subject-verb agreement.				
Uses quotation marks to signal spoken words.				
Uses a capital letter to begin dialogue.				
Uses a comma to signal a speaker tag.				

The best part of the essay is ...

A suggestion to make the essay even better is ...

Name

Handout 34A: Writing Planner

Directions: Use this graphic organizer to plan a response to the End-of-Module Task.

	E	Establish	How will you orient your reader to the situation?
	S	Setting	When and where does the story take place?
	C	Characters	Who is the story about, and what do they want?
	A	Action	What events happen, and how do the characters respond?
	P	Problem	What prevents the main character from getting what they want?
	E	Ending	What is the resolution to the problem?

Name

Handout 35A: Thoughtshot–Dialogue–Snapshot Chart

Directions: Brainstorm several ideas for each part of the chart that you might want to include in your exploded moment narrative.

THOUGHTSHOT: What do the characters think or feel?	DIALOGUE: What do the characters say (dialogue)?

SNAPSHOT: Use sensory details to describe the scene.				
Seeing	Hearing	Tasting	Touching	Smelling

Name

Handout 35B:
End-of-Module Task Checklist

Directions:

1. Use this checklist as you review your completed letter. Mark + for "yes" and Δ for "not yet."
2. Then give your letter and the checklist to a peer, who will also review the checklist.
3. Make necessary revisions.
4. Give the completed letter and checklist to your teacher.

Reading Comprehension	Self +/ Δ	Peer +/ Δ	Teacher +/ Δ
• I use details about immigration and finding a new home to create a piece of realistic fiction. • I write from the point of view of character we have read about.			
Structure			
• I respond to all parts of the prompt.			
• I introduce a narrator and/or character(s). • I organize my events in a natural order.			
• I establish setting and conflict for my narrative or story.			
• I provide a sense of closure at the end.			
• I use time words and phrases to tell my reader when events happen.			

Development			
• I use dialogue and description to develop events and characters.			
• I use description to develop events and characters.			
Style			
• I use vocabulary words that are appropriate to the topic.			
• I use and circle at least three new vocabulary words.			
• My writing is appropriate for the purpose and audience of the task.			
Conventions			
• I ensure subject-verb agreement.			
• I use commas and quotation marks in dialogue.			
• I form and use possessives.			
• I use at least one abstract noun.			
• I form and use irregular verbs.			
• I form and use regular and irregular plural nouns.			
Writing Process			
• I use a Writing Planner to organize my ideas.			
• I provide thoughtful feedback in peer revision.			
• I use feedback in peer revision.			
Total number of +'s:			

Name

Handout 35C:
End-of-Module Task Revision Checklist

Directions:

1. Exchange End-of-Module Task narratives with a partner.

2. Read your partner's narrative all the way through before making comments or suggestions.

3. Use proofreading marks to annotate the narrative, and indicate punctuation corrections.

4. Write "irr pl n" in the margin next to sentences that do <u>not</u> use the correct plural form of an irregular noun.

5. Write "irr" in the margin next to sentences that do <u>not</u> use the correct form of an irregular verb.

6. Write "abst. n!" in the margin where you notice the writer used an abstract noun.

7. Complete the checklist below.

8. Return the narrative and checklist to your partner.

9. Review and revise your own narrative, using your partner's feedback.

Writer:_____   Editor:_____

In the narrative, the writer ...	Yes	Sometimes	Rarely	Not Present
Uses possessives correctly.				
Ensures subject-verb agreement.				
Uses quotation marks to signal spoken words.				
Uses a capital letter to begin dialogue.				
Uses a comma to signal a speaker tag.				
Uses an abstract noun.				
Correctly uses irregular plural nouns.				
Correctly uses irregular verbs.				

The best part of the essay is ...

A suggestion to make the essay even better is ...

Name

Volume of Reading Reflection Questions

Text: _____

Author: _____

Topic: _____

Genre/Type of Book: _____

Share your knowledge about immigration by responding to the questions below.

Informational Text

1. **Wonder:** What is one question about immigration you think this text will answer?

2. **Organize:** Pick two or three key details the author presents about immigration. What is the main idea represented by the key details?

3. **Reveal:** What is one challenge about immigration that the author discusses in this text? How do immigrants overcome this challenge?

4. **Distill:** Did the author have a favorable view of immigration? Provide evidence from the text to support your response.

5. **Know:** How does the information in this text compare to what you have already learned about immigration? Provide at least two examples of information that is the same and/or different.

6. **Vocabulary:** Write two important vocabulary words and definitions that you learned in this text in your Vocabulary Journal. What makes them important words to know when you read about immigration?

Literary Text

1. **Wonder:** What do you notice after closely examining the front and back covers or after reading the first couple pages of this text?

2. **Organize:** Choose three important actions of characters in the story. How does each action add to, or shape, the story?

3. **Reveal:** Choose one character in the story, and think about their point of view. Do you agree with what they say and do in the story? Explain your thinking.

4. **Distill:** What is the central message in this story? Provide evidence from the text to support your response. Is the central message similar to other immigration stories you read in class?

5. **Know:** How has this story added to what you know about immigration?

6. **Vocabulary:** Write two important vocabulary words and definitions that you learned in this text in your Vocabulary Journal. What makes them important words to understand and know when you read about immigration?

WIT & WISDOM FAMILY TIP SHEET

WHAT IS MY THIRD GRADE STUDENT LEARNING IN MODULE 3?

Wit & Wisdom is our English curriculum. It builds knowledge of key topics in history, science, and literature through the study of excellent texts. By reading and responding to stories and nonfiction texts, we will build knowledge of the following topics:

Module 1: The Sea

Module 2: Outer Space

Module 3: A New Home

Module 4: Artists Make Art

In the Module 3, A New Home, students will explore the immigrant experience through the lens of stories. We will ask: How do stories help us understand immigrants' experiences?

OUR CLASS WILL READ THESE BOOKS:

Picture Books (Literary)

- *Grandfather's Journey*, Allen Say
- *Tea with Milk*, Allen Say
- *The Keeping Quilt*, Patricia Polacco
- *Family Pictures*, Carmen Lomas Garza

Picture Books (Informational)

- *Coming to America: The Story of Immigration*, Betsy Maestro

OUR CLASS WILL READ THIS STORY:

- "Two Places to Call Home," Jody Kapp

OUR CLASS WILL EXAMINE THESE PHOTOGRAPHS:

- *The Steerage*, Alfred Stieglitz
- "Fleeing Hitler: Refugee Children from England Arrive in New York during World War II, 18th July 1940," Getty Images

OUR CLASS WILL EXAMINE THIS ARCHITECTURE:

- "Liberty Enlightening the World," Frédéric Auguste Bartholdi

- Gateway Arch, Eero Saarinen

- "Guide to Visiting the Washington Monument," Robert Mills

OUR CLASS WILL WATCH THESE VIDEOS:

- "Día de los Muertos Festival 2015–Artist Talk by Carmen Lomas Garza 1," Smithsonian National Museum of the American Indian

OUR CLASS WILL LISTEN TO THESE HISTORICAL ACCOUNTS:

- "Morris Remembers the Steamship," Ellis Island Oral History Collection

- "William Remembers the Storm," Ellis Island Oral History Collection

- "Oral History Library," The Statue of Liberty–Ellis Island Foundation, Inc.

OUR CLASS WILL ASK THESE QUESTIONS:

1 What challenges do immigrants face in a new country?

2 Why do people immigrate to America?

3 How do immigrants respond to challenges in a new country?

QUESTIONS TO ASK AT HOME

As you read with your Grade 3 student, ask:

- What is the essential meaning, or most important message, in this book?

BOOKS TO READ AT HOME

- *At Ellis Island: A History in Many Voices*, Louise Peacock

- *Ellis Island*, Elaine Landau

- *Four Feet, Two Sandals*, Karen Lynn Williams

- *Immigrant Kids*, Russell Freedman

- *In the Year of the Boar and Jackie Robinson*, Betty Bao Lord

- *Paper Son: Lee's Journey to America*, Helen Foster James

- *The Great Migration: An American Story*, Walter Dean Myers and Jacob Lawrence

- *Tucky Jo and Little Heart*, Patricia Polacco

- *Lowji Discovers America*, Candace Fleming

- *Peppe the Lamplighter*, Elisa Bartone

- *The Memory Coat*, Elvira Woodruff

- *Laila's Lunchbox*, Reem Faruqi
- *Katrina's Wish*, Jeannie Mobley
- *Landed*, Milly Lee
- *Rebekkah's Journey: A World War II Refugee Story*, Ann E. Burg
- *Hannah's Journal: The Story of an Immigrant Girl*, Marissa Moss

IDEAS FOR TALKING ABOUT THE IMMIGRANT EXPERIENCE

Share your family's history. Consider sharing:

- Your family's country of ancestry on a map or globe.
- Customs, traditions, and food from your family's country of origin.
- Folktales and music from your family's country of origin.

Learn more about the Statue of Liberty and other monuments. Consider:

- Taking a virtual tour of the Statue of Liberty.
- Visiting a local monument.

CREDITS

Great Minds® has made every effort to obtain permission for the reprinting of all copyrighted material. If any owner of copyrighted material is not acknowledged herein, please contact Great Minds® for proper acknowledgment in all future editions and reprints of this module.

- All material from the *Common Core State Standards for English Language Arts & Literacy in History/Social Studies, Science, and Technical Subjects* © Copyright 2010 National Governors Association Center for Best Practices and Council of Chief State School Officers. All rights reserved.

- All images are used under license from Shutterstock.com unless otherwise noted.

- Handout 15A: "Two Places to Call Home" by Jody Kapp from Ladybug magazine, March 2007. Text copyright © 2007 by Carus Publishing Company. Reprinted by permission of Cricket Media. All Cricket Media material is copyrighted by Carus Publishing d/b/a Cricket Media, and/or various authors and illustrators. Any commercial use or distribution of material without permission is strictly prohibited. Please visit **http://www.cricketmedia.com/info/licensing2** for licensing and **http://www.cricketmedia.com** for subscriptions.

- For updated credit information, please visit **http://witeng.link/credits**.

ACKNOWLEDGMENTS

Great Minds® Staff

The following writers, editors, reviewers, and support staff contributed to the development of this curriculum.

Karen Aleo, Elizabeth Bailey, Ashley Bessicks, Sarah Brenner, Ann Brigham, Catherine Cafferty, Sheila Byrd-Carmichael, Lauren Chapalee, Emily Climer, Rebecca Cohen, Elaine Collins, Julia Dantchev, Beverly Davis, Shana Dinner de Vaca, Kristy Ellis, Moira Clarkin Evans, Marty Gephart, Mamie Goodson, Nora Graham, Lindsay Griffith, Lorraine Griffith, Christina Gonzalez, Emily Gula, Brenna Haffner, Joanna Hawkins, Elizabeth Haydel, Sarah Henchey, Trish Huerster, Ashley Hymel, Carol Jago, Mica Jochim, Jennifer Johnson, Mason Judy, Sara Judy, Lior Klirs, Shelly Knupp, Liana Krissoff, Sarah Kushner, Suzanne Lauchaire, Diana Leddy, David Liben, Farren Liben, Brittany Lowe, Whitney Lyle, Stephanie Kane-Mainier, Liz Manolis, Jennifer Marin, Audrey Mastroleo, Maya Marquez, Susannah Maynard, Cathy McGath, Emily McKean, Andrea Minich, Rebecca Moore, Lynne Munson, Carol Paiva, Michelle Palmieri, Tricia Parker, Marya Myers Parr, Meredith Phillips, Eden Plantz, Shilpa Raman, Rachel Rooney, Jennifer Ruppel, Julie Sawyer-Wood, Nicole Shivers, Danielle Shylit, Rachel Stack, Amelia Swabb, Vicki Taylor, Melissa Thomson, Lindsay Tomlinson, Tsianina Tovar, Sarah Turnage, Melissa Vail, Keenan Walsh, Michelle Warner, Julia Wasson, Katie Waters, Sarah Webb, Lynn Welch, Yvonne Guerrero Welch, Amy Wierzbicki, Margaret Wilson, Sarah Woodard, Lynn Woods, and Rachel Zindler

Colleagues and Contributors

We are grateful for the many educators, writers, and subject-matter experts who made this program possible.

David Abel, Robin Agurkis, Sarah Ambrose, Rebeca Barroso, Julianne Barto, Amy Benjamin, Andrew Biemiller, Charlotte Boucher, Adam Cardais, Eric Carey, Jessica Carloni, Dawn Cavalieri, Janine Cody, Tequila Cornelious, David Cummings, Matt Davis, Thomas Easterling, Jeanette Edelstein, Sandra Engleman, Charles Fischer, Kath Gibbs, Natalie Goldstein, Laurie Gonsoulin, Dennis Hamel, Kristen Hayes, Steve Hettleman, Cara Hoppe, Libby Howard, Gail Kearns, Lisa King, Sarah Kopec, Andrew Krepp, Shannon Last, Ted MacInnis, Christina Martire, Alisha McCarthy, Cindy Medici, Brian Methe, Ivonne Mercado, Patricia Mickelberry, Jane Miller, Cathy Newton, Turi Nilsson, Julie Norris, Tara O'Hare, Galemarie Ola, Tamara Otto, Christine Palmtag, Dave Powers, Jeff Robinson, Karen Rollhauser, Tonya Romayne, Emmet Rosenfeld, Mike Russoniello, Deborah Samley, Casey Schultz, Renee Simpson, Rebecca Sklepovich, Kim Taylor, Tracy Vigliotti, Charmaine Whitman, Glenda Wisenburn-Burke, and Howard Yaffe

Early Adopters

The following early adopters provided invaluable insight and guidance for Wit & Wisdom:

- Bourbonnais School District 53 • Bourbonnais, IL
- Coney Island Prep Middle School • Brooklyn, NY
- Gate City Charter School for the Arts • Merrimack, NH
- Hebrew Academy for Special Children • Brooklyn, NY
- Paris Independent Schools • Paris, KY
- Saydel Community School District • Saydel, IA
- Strive Collegiate Academy • Nashville, TN
- Valiente College Preparatory Charter School • South Gate, CA
- Voyageur Academy • Detroit, MI

Design Direction provided by Alton Creative, Inc.

Project management support, production design, and copyediting services provided by ScribeConcepts.com

Copyediting services provided by Fine Lines Editing

Product management support provided by Sandhill Consulting